I0083271

Unconditional Election

Unconditional Election
Poems

H. C. Kim

The Hermit Kingdom Press
Cheltenham   Seoul   Bangalore   Cebu City

Unconditional Election: Poems

All Rights Reserved © 2006 by H. C. Kim

No part of this book may be reproduced or transmitted in any form or by any means, graphic, electronic, or mechanical, including photocopying, recording, taping, or by any information storage retrieval system, without the permission in writing from the publisher.

For information address:

The Hermit Kingdom Press
12325 Imperial Highway, Suite 156
Norwalk, California 90650
United States of America
info@TheHermitKingdomPress.com

http://www.TheHermitKingdomPress.com

ISBN: 1-59689-057-6

Library of Congress Cataloging-in-Publication Data

Kim, H. C. (Heerak Christian)
  Unconditional election : poems / H.C. Kim.
      p. cm.
  ISBN 1-59689-057-6 (pbk. : alk. paper)
  I. Title.
  PS3611.I4544U53 2006
  811'.6--dc22

                                           2006015369

Dedicated to the Memory of

Dr. James Montgomery Boice (1938 - 2000)

Pastor of Tenth Presbyterian Church, Philadelphia

"A man with God is always in the majority."

John Knox, the founder of the Presbyterian Church,

Otherwise known as The Church of Scotland

Contents

Contents

Preface

Often, we try to make sense our experiences, particularly tragedies that confront us. It is at such times that we confront the divine and understand that what stands outside of us gives us faith and that the world around us is filled with much meaning.

H. C. Kim
Easter, 2006
Heidelberg
Germany

Unconditional Election

"Bell"

There's a bell
Perched way up there
For all to see
All over the vast campus

But silent is this bell
That refuses to ring
And break the silence
That dominates the campus

Isolated
In loneliness
Like the students
Who walk circumspect

Afraid to break
The written law
Made at every whim
With no regard to personhood

Humanity of students
Who are left dangling
In a place
They can't claim as their own

Lifeless building
All over
Accompanied by stern looks
Bell is afraid to ring

"Cobbled Stones"

Cobbled stones marked the way
Like the golden road of myths
Magical incantation scribbled
Beyond the cobbled pathway

I walked and walked
Feeling the stones below me
In search of magic
The ancient stones promised

But there was only emptiness
Miles and miles of cobbled stones
Extending on and on
Into the sunset

"Baghdad Christmas"

It's Christmas here
In the war zone
Where bullets fly
Gun shots are heard
Despondency is felt
Cries are seen
Hope nearly evaporating

It's Christmas here
In the terror frontier
Where people die
Merciless sun beats
Sands flying everywhere
Snow nowhere to be seen
Happiness fleeting

It's Christmas here
In the city of Baghdad
Where we had our war
Destruction
Death
Revenge
Justice rendered

It's Christmas here
A place of our penitence
Where we atone
Collect alms
Try to rebuild
Make up for all the destruction
Staying not to abandon

"Disneyland"

I went to Disneyland
To find something
I don't know
Quite what

Maybe I went there
To escape
The world
That I considered my prison

Was I searching for love?
Real love?
I cannot say
But it is a lovely place I guess

Did I fall into a created world?
A world within a world
Within a world within a world
Someone put me there?

I could not feel anything
But deep unhappiness
Even as I pretended
To be in the happiest place on earth

I knew I had become a pawn
In a game that I did not create
But became a part of
Maybe I even consented to it

"Beat the Colored Boy"

Beat the colored boy!
I heard shouted out.

I turned around to see who
Could cry out such an abomination.

I looked and looked
But only beheld my friends.

They stood there silently
With their lips firmly closed.

Where did the cry come from?
I was so sure I heard it.

It was then I realized –
Silence shouted louder than any sound.

"Don't Diss Me"

Don't Diss Me
I heard the prophet say
For there are consequences
I saw the tears in his eyes

For the Almighty don't take kindly
To the humiliation of his representative
I heard the prophet's entreaty
And wondered what he meant

I ignored his words
Thinking they were ramblings of a fool
And taunted him
And laughed and laughed and laughed

Two months later
I remembered the words
Those of the prophet the fool
And his entreaty

As I took my mom
To the hospital ward
For her follow-up check-up
After a cancer diagnosis

"Black History"

The History of Black People
A People of Color
Relegated to the Corner
Othered reality

Why?
Because it is inconvenient
To study the history of the Othered
To research to find the reality

Why?
Because it is offensive
Personally to those who are convicted
Of the wrongs committed in this country

Why?
Because there is no money in it
To study people who were enslaved
And dehumanized

Why?
Because glory does not await
Those who pursue excellence
In the study of the people of color

Why?
Because there is segregation
In the minds of those
Who have desegregated themselves outwardly

"Empty Room"

Room is empty
Books have no friends
They are left on the shelf
To rot

Where are the people
For whom this building was made
Books are left untouched
Unread

You hear only
The ringing of keys
Of custodians
Measured walk of librarians

The building is empty
The spirit of the writers
Slain in the name
Of peace

Inspiration left wanting
For professors who carry the routine
Students who try to get tuition's worth
Staff who just work

Creativity
You cannot find
For there is facism
Of the academic kind

"Fancy"

Fancy
Everything is fancy
Everyone is fancy
All I see is fancy

I am wearing fancy clothes
They are wearing fancy clothes
You are wearing fancy clothes
Only fancy clothes

Fancy food
I see everywhere
Carried by fancy-looking waiters
And fancy-want-to-be waitresses

Fancy
I am surrounded by fancy
Fanciness in its glory
And I am in the middle of it

I feel fancy
And am swept away by fanciness
I know I am in a fancy universe
Fancy beyond all possibility

And I think to myself
What it would be like
To have less fancy
And a bit more reality

"Dr. Martin Luther King"

What would be different had Martin not died?
The good o' Doctor he would be right now.
But lo and behold!
He died a young age,
Depriving the young of his leadership and wisdom.

What would be different now had Luther lived?
Centered in a reformist attitude and practice
That changed a generation.
Could he not have changed many more generations?
What is lost without him?

What would be different had King not died?
Would we have the ideology of the King on earth?
The principles of Jesus of Nazareth
Who practiced Open Table Fellowship with righteousness
Could have made a positive impact, no?

What would be different had Dr. Martin Luther King lived?
We will never know because he's dead.
We are left with increasing problems:
End to affirmative action,
Rising minimization of the people of color.

"Fear"

Students run in fear
Rather walk in fear
Maybe more accurate to say
Gingerly take measured steps in fear

For they don't know
Which police will get them
Feminazi police
Political correctness police

Students walk in fear
Without a spark in their eyes
Their youth killed
By the spirit of academia

That has become a policing agency
Of thoughts unspoken
Words expressed
Ideas generated

Creativity is the enemy
Of the spirit of academia
The unwritten rule goes
You need to tow our line

"Election"

Electing against something
Not really for anything
Out of our wounded pride
Because of peer pressure
Without thinking
Not feeling the Other's pain
Where are we
That we have come to this
We elect
Based on our fear
On account of a hearsay
What we think we saw
And the reality eludes
Electing something
Anything

"Fireworks"

I saw the fireworks in the sky
And was amazed
By the beauty of it all

It was out of this world
Or the closest I will come to it
And I stood in awe

All alone
Until a hand reached for me
Out of nowhere

But it was not unexpected
And I can't say unplanned
But I feigned a pleasant surprise

And drank in the sweet words
As warmness pressed my hand
As I felt the coldness in my heart

I stared at the sky in front of me
Fireworks exploding in the sky
And I felt special

I knew it wasn't real
Deep inside I knew
But I wanted to imagine

What could be
What could have been
What I did not want to miss

"Hurricane Katrina"

Out of nowhere
The mistress of destruction
Barged in

With her awesome power,
Fury and destruction.
As if in a jealous rage

To settle scores
For a love unfulfilled,
Hurricane Katrina

Showed no mercy
And continued to cry for blood,
Death and destruction.

Who can understand her rage?
New Orleans suffered
In puzzlement and helplessly.

Blows after blows came
Even when New Orleans slept;
There was no humane mercy.

"Her Dream"

I knew that she was dreaming
Although she was wide awake

She was living a dream
Perhaps she thought it was her own

Like a child before Nicholas Day
Who had not been told the facts

She carried a hidden smile
An anticipation of something fantastic

She may have thought herself happy
To be in a dream world

I could not shake her
I did not want to give her the facts

It was nice to see her happy
Thinking herself to be happy

For I wanted her to follow her happiness
Wherever that will take her

She is old enough to decide
What makes her happy

I stood by
As she dreamed her dream

Thinking she was living
A fantastic dream of happiness

I stood by because I knew
She did not want me to be in her dream

"Model Immigrant"

Yessir,
I'm a model immigrant
An' I keep me mouth shut
Understand
You don't wanna hear me speak
For I'm yellow and uncouth
I'm an immigrant from far, far away
An' proud of my culture, history, and people
But I'll keep me mouth shut
'Cause who wanna hear yellow lips painted red speak

Yessir,
I'm a model immigrant
An' know nothin' I say
Will sound right
I will keep me mouth shut
An' say nothin'
I'll be invisible
Just the way you like
I can say nothin' right
I understand

"Here"

She asked herself
How did I get here?
With him by my side
As if in destiny

She wondered
If she were really lucky
Like many fake people
Said she was

Or if she was pushed
Into a corner
To a box
Which now began to suffocate

Even as she smiled
Fake smiles for fake people
Who expected the smile
And knew they were fake

She asked herself
Where am I going?
With him by my side
To a fake place?

"Organize"

How quickly they organize
As if guided by some god of direction.

You say this,
And I will say this.

Surely, they did not plan in advance.
But they are like conjoined twins.

I will use my right hand.
You use your left.

We will work together
And we will win.

Credo is newly fashioned by them;
Religion is created.

They organize so efficiently
For a purpose they both understand,

To destroy
And to profit from another's sorrow.

"Hunger"

I see the hunger in their eyes
For something substantial
Not merely mechanical
Nor superficial

Not just the mechanics of lovemaking
Devoid of life-blood
And human spirit
Merely feeding the flesh

But the content
Behind the act
The spirit that gives meaning
Love that is expressed

Both in words
Deeds
And in pleasant nothings
Full of meaning

Not just the act
Like the way birds do it
Or the buzzing bees
But what makes them

Human
Full of life-blood
Bound by spirit of humanness
Engulfed in centuries of meaning

"Thanks"

Thanks
I would like to say
But so hard to verbalize

Thanks
I think
I feel

Thanks
I know I should express
But can't for some reason

Thanks
I won't utter
I can't bear to hear myself voice

Thanks
Mine to hide
Deep in my heart

Thanks
Saying it will weaken me
I won't be feeble

Thanks
You'll never hear me say
Although you deserve to know it

Thanks
I will cry out in silence
Alone in privacy

Thanks
I do feel
But just for me to know

"I Can't See Me"

I can't see me
I learned the hard way

I thought I was like
Those whom I saw

For I can't see myself
And I don't bother with mirrors

I thought I was just like them
Participated in all their amusements

Thinking I was one of them
And will always be a part of them

Then, I realized I was different
Not because I saw myself

But because I saw how they treated him
Who looked like me, my father, my brother

I understood that they hated my kind
Yellow in color

I was the exception
Which assuaged their conscience

As they taunted my kind
To whose group I belong because of my skin

I will always look like him
Him who is taunted

But often I forgot that I look like him
And joined in the taunts and the laughs

"White Christmas"

Trees covered in snow
Pristine
Unadulterated
Like in the pictures

Winds blowing
Requiring mittens
Fuzzy hat
And a cushiony jacket

A Christmas tree
With lots of lighting
Shining through the wide window
Details blurred by falling snow

How would that feel?
I wonder
Trying to remember
The White Christmas of yester-years

"Is There God?"

Is there God?
I heard the paralytic ask
For I suffer
In my uselessness

The prophet replied
There is God
For you suffer
And doubt God's presence

Tis' the proof
There is God
For you deserve to suffer
Doubting the existence of God

What?
I heard the paralytic protest
I would believe
Were I whole

You are whole
The prophet replied
I see a wonderful person
With great potential

God sees you
As someone who can be his own light
You have been unconditionally elected
To be paralytic and beautiful

"Jeremiah Is Wrong"

I am convinced that Jeremiah is wrong
To prophecy the destruction of Israel
A believing nation
At the hand of Babylonians
Who neither love God nor worship him

Who does this Jeremiah think he is?
Okay, he's a prophet, so what?
That doesn't excuse the crassness
The offensiveness, all the hateful speech
Of proclaiming destruction, talk of violence

What if he is an inspired representative of God?
It doesn't give him excuse
To upset the polite folk
Who just want to live their normal lives
Without controversy or annoyance

Jeremiah is wrong
To barge in on the king
And tell him that he will be captured
The king who worships God
By a king who never worshipped God

What is he thinking?
Is he out of his mind?
Who cares if he is chosen to speak for God?
He has no right to speak
Such violent words and break peace

Then, I realized
The Babylonians are at the city gates
And news has spread throughout my city
Jerusalem the chosen city
That Babylonians are about to destroy it completely

Maybe Jeremiah is not wrong after all
Maybe I should have listened to him
Who knows
Maybe Jerusalem will not be destroyed
Later historians will confirm the facts

"Karaoke"

I remember the songs we sang
In that small room of music
A makeshift recording studio
In a far away land
With my foreign best friend

Whose thoughts were back home
Where his lovely fiancée awaited
For his return
Like Penelope
Her true love

We sang our hearts out
Him for his fiancée
Me for my land of childhood
Where the small music room
Unlike any we've seen back there

An hour and a half passed by
With songs recorded on an empty cassette
Provided by the karaoke room
Two best buddies croaking their voice
Without shame or embarrassment

One for his lovely girl
The other for the childhood he remembered
Both thinking of what's dear
Voice going hoarse
Songs chosen on a whim

There is a cassette to prove it
That day in the karaoke room
In a small corner building
In the bustle of Seoul
Where two best buddies sang together for the last time

"Meaning"

She searched for meaning
In the midst of all the confusion
What just happened?
How did I end up here?

Things seemed to crash together
Like a racing car colliding
Hitting a tree by the road
Everything dismantled

She felt like that
The mess after the race car crash
Her life was broken
How did I get here?

She remembered getting into the car
The racing car was fancy and shiny
And she felt she could get a ride
That would mark her life as special

But she didn't remember
The moment she made the decision
Through a conscious questioning
She just got in the car on a whim

And now
Here she was
Trying to pick up the pieces
After the crash

"Mickey Mouse"

I met the Mickey Mouse
Yes, in person, yesterday
And he spoke to me

That was when my world ended
Mickey Mouse isn't supposed to speak
He is beyond speech

But there he was speaking
Friendly words
Funny sayings

And I knew the voice
Behind the mask
It was shall-I-say a friend

That day a big part of me died
As I smiled for the cameras
And the one behind the mask

Mickey Mouse never will be
Magical for me
Because I know he is only a cover

"Not Your Church"

Not your church
I heard the prophet say
But it is God's church
As if he exulted in slapping their faces
The wealthy of Los Angeles

What did this guy mean?
To barge in on a wealthy church
Without the humility owed to the rich
He should just sit there
Content to be among those rolling in dough

Not your church
The prophet repeated
As if he owned the place
This is God's church
He said out loud

Annoyed faces of the wealthy
Who refuse to get involved
In religious arguments of the day
Seemed truly annoyed
By the unpleasant intrusion

Doesn't this guy know
The prophet who dressed in a cheap suit
It is not appropriate to upset polite society
With all the talk of God and his demands
The rich don't come to church for him

It's a social club you see
Where pleasant folk drink tea together
Talk about little nothings
Nothing too controversial
Like a country club

All this talk of religious duty
Needing to spend personal money
For Christian missions
And pro-Christian legislation
Doesn't this prophet know how inappropriate it is?

"Pencil"

Pencil scribbles
In frustration
As a doctoral student
Tries to fish for meaning

Those books piled up
Read and reread
Give no direction
He is bored and asks

Why am I here?
What is the meaning of life?
What is this all for?
And he hits the table

With the tip of his pen
Silent noise
Of sharp protest
At his own life

He feels is slipping away
Along with his dreams
Hopes and fears
Promises for tomorrow

He tries to convince himself
The pencil will set him free
Eventually
So he hopes

"Prophet of Doom"

I saw the prophet of doom
In his moments of weakness
When he doubted
The prophecy of disaster
Which the LORD had given him

I asked him
Why do you look perturbed
And doubt
A shell of a prophet
You appear

I cannot bear the horror
The vision of terror
The LORD gave me in my dream
Little babies dying
As the doom falls from the sky

What do you mean?
I asked
Horrified
Trying to understand
Checking to see if I heard right

The prophecy
The prophet said
Is of doom and destruction
What I have seen is death after death
Young and the old

Weak and the strong
Rich and the poor
All dying together
In a horrible visitation of the LORD
In His wrath to judge

I told the prophet
I don't know much
And I'm only a child
But if the LORD gave you the prophecy
Trust in His righteousness and be bold

"Raised Hands"

Hands are raised
Like they never were before
In this land
Where this is rarely seen

The young
The proud
And the defiant
Collective

Each looking at the other
Fearful at first
But conceding support
Turning enthusiastic

Like the music that shook the hall
Moments before causing dance
Now hands are raised
In silent remembrance

Looks gathered
Into the centre of the dance floor
Where two hands greet
One black and the other yellow

"Samson"

Samson asked himself
Why did the LORD choose me
To be a prophet-warrior
For His people?

For I am of unclean lips
Unclean heart
Unclean behavior
Unclean thoughts

The LORD could have chosen
Someone far more worthy
Far more polished
Far more pure

Yet He chose me
To be His prophet
To deliver His message
To execute His plans

Why has the LORD chosen me?
An unconditional election
For I meet none of the LORD's requirements
But I will obey

"Silky"

Silky
Her hair glistened
Under the artificial light
Shining like a sun
In the dingy room
In the middle of the night

Silky
Her hair flowed
Like the satin sheets
On the display window
In New Delhi
Way out East

Silky
Her hair felt
Between my fingers
Like gentle flowing waters
Passing in a waterfall
In Ein Gedi

Silky
Her hair is remembered
In empty thoughts
That pass by during the day
Accompanied by memory
Of her smile

"Strike the Prophet"

I heard of a new game
Called strike the prophet
And the game is like it's called
You go and strike the prophet

And I remembered the story of Elisha
The consequence of taunting
By boys not yet in the age of reason
Struck dead by the living God

And wondered what would become
Of them who abused
The prophet
Unconditionally elected by God

H. C. Kim

"The Anointed"

He can't be anointed by God
I doubted the prophet
Who rambled and cussed
Designating an idiot the anointed

The Almighty raises up the fool
To humble the smart folk
I heard the prophet proclaim
Who the fool I asked

You the fool not
Because you are wise in your own eyes
Said the prophet
And insulted me to my face

Who the fool I asked again
He the fool whom you think is the fool
Said the prophet
And laughed with tears in his eyes

A joker's laugh
Like in the Batman movie
Yet I am unsettled
For he appeared dead serious

"The Book"

I searched for the book
That was to unlock
The door to answers
For the many questions
That plagued my being

I conducted a basic search
In the library catalogue
Thinking that I would find this book
But the screen returned
Only an empty screen

I thought that the librarian could help
So I rushed to the help desk
As quietly as my agitated frame allowed
But the librarian shook her head
And feigned ignorance

I did not know what to do
So I buried myself
On the comfortable library chair
Thinking I might have an epiphany
And be guided to the book

But I knew as I sat there
In despondent relaxation
That I knew not where to look
For the book unconditionally chosen
But elusive beyond comprehension

"The Cart"

Cart is being pushed
By a bored librarian
Who wonders
Where all the students are

The library is empty
For God's sake
She says
As the cart rolls along

Less work for me
She tries to assure herself
And give her work meaning
Silence only broken by the cart

It would be nice to have a few students
She can't help thinking
So I will understand and see
My presence here has meaning

But she only hears the cart
That breaks the silence
In the room devoid of human spirit
The empty chamber of her heart

"The Conspiracy"

He heard the conspiracy
And smiled because he found it funny
Amusing and entertaining
Why not?
He asked himself
And took part

A bunch of students
Playing the practical joke
Isn't it?
He tried to convince himself
And even took joy in his participation
Thinking it was harmless

Then, things happened
Their conspiracy worked
The target was secured
And the victory was won
Now, the handcuffs awaited him
The one against whom the conspiracy stood

He wasn't sure what to think
But he felt himself too vested
To step in to stop the ruse
A trick that turned into an evil treat
For those who hated him
For the color of his skin

He tried to ignore it
The impending doom
Well, for the target of conspiracy
And tried to assuage his guilt
Walked into the bathroom to brush his teeth
And saw in the mirror the object of the conspiracy

"The Conversation"

I wonder what they are saying
In the midst of the din
Created by hip-hop background
Talking and talking away
I don't think it's about hip-hop
Method
Jealousy
Don't know
Can only catch two words
The professor trying to impress
The protégé seeking to seem interested
Academic tutelage forming
In a democratic society
Devoid of patronage
Even TA's are motivated by capitalism
Artificial production of knowledge
Institution to maintain capital system
As much to perpetuate knowledge
Creative thinking?
Wouldn't be prudent
The protégé nods
Doesn't raise her voice a bit
And there is only acquiescence
No disagreement

"The Day of the Lord"

I heard the prophet say
The Day of the Lord is coming
And wondered if it were true
If there were such a judgment in store
If there even was a god

I heard the prophet scream
Like a madman
Out of a looney bin
His face turning red
Spit coming out between his screams

I watched the prophet
And did not know whether to laugh
Cry, smile, stay still, or jump around
He looked so sincere
Yet I could not believe him

There can't be such a day
The Day of the Lord
That brings destruction
Death of the innocent
Well at least in my eyes

The Day of the Lord is coming!
The prophet would not relent
But screamed for an hour
And I did not know if I was mad
Or felt pity for this rambling soul

I thought about the supernatural
If tragedy were planned
Acts of a god
Rather than chanced occurrence
Just plain bad luck

The Day of the Lord is imminent!
The prophet spoke
As if speaking to me
And I felt a chill go along my spine
For against my wishes, I believed

"The Gift"

I wanted to give a gift
To a friend of many years.

What would be meaningful?
I asked myself.

What will make her happy?
I thought out loud.

I was convinced
The best gift was love.

Then I saw her
And realized otherwise.

What she needed
Was not love.

She was not ready for it.
She probably did not want it.

I understood
She needed confidence.

Arduously I worked
To give her confidence.

That would be for her
My gift of love.

"The Old Lady"

The old lady
Sits there on the sofa
The most comfortable chair
In this whole vast library
And she pretends to read
But we know what she's doing
She's a sociologist
Studying the social behavior
Of stressed out students
Trying to make the grade
But she pretends badly
Nonchalantly
That she's working too
But she looks too comfortable
Disinterested in what she's holding
So she gives herself away
She is bored with life
Her own that is
She has taken an interest
In all the students
With stressed out body language
Intensely writing away

"The Persian"

A Persian student sits
Holding his newspaper
Headlined
One Step Away
As he ignores
His two big MCAT books
His mind is not
In the medical school he desires
But in the war scenario
Of Iran the Defiant
Which just launched
Two missiles in war games
One avoiding radar detection
Another underwater missile
More powerful than any of its kind
America owns in its whole war arsenal
Does he want a war?
So Iran can prove its worth
Who knows?
He is fixated on the headline
One Step Away

"The Photo of the Sea"

I looked at my photo of the sea
I could remember when I was there
Walking on the sandy beach
Looking far away in the distance

The sun shining above in the sky
I could feel the wind on my face
And I counted the clouds above
And heard the birds fly and sing

The photo looked alive
Maybe because it was a digital one
Spread out large
Before my computer screen

It's like watching TV
And I remember this view
In real life
But can't remember what I thought then

This picture only has the sea
No person on the photo
I was looking towards the sea
And wanted only to capture nature

I wonder now
What I was thinking
Maybe if I let a human in then
I could now remember

All I remember is the sea
The smell of the sea water
Sound of sea birds
And the cloud in the sky

"The Prize"

He sat there
Right in front
Of the beautiful woman
He had won as a prize

He looked there
At his plate
Which contained fancy food
The most expensive on the menu

He thought there
Reminiscing of the days of youth
When he used to eat simple rice porridge
In his mother's kitchen

He saw there
His dainty girl
Taking small bites
Chewing in silence

He wondered there
If this was all there was
For which he had fought so hard
To win his prize

"The Runner"

He runs
Across the library
Like it's his own living room
Perhaps he should not be here
So often all the time
An Asian student
Studying for his MCATs
Doesn't see the students
Quietly trying to study around him
He is absorbed in his little world
And the library has become his home
His living room and recreational space
For him to study is his life
For what?
Only he knows?
Maybe he doesn't even know

"The Sit"

She sat there
And talked on and on
About the deficiencies
That she noticed

She criticized
With a passion
That hid her true heart
Of affection for him

He sat there
Not quite knowing what to do
Desiring her
But resenting her words

She talked on and on
With a concern
That was true
That linked her heart to his

But he did not understand
Her love and affection
He merely heard the words spoken
And misunderstood her intention

They parted cordially
As friends
But he knew the hurt was too deep
It could not be what he desired

She felt a connection
She thought she saw
Because of a reaction
She solicited from his composure

She knew
Emotion was better than none
Even when it was resentment
And she hoped and smiled

"The Tale"

I couldn't get the tale
Out of my mind
The one which I heard
About two brothers

Was it true?
Can a selfish brother
Show selflessness
In his own cruel way?

Cruel to all parties
Perhaps not to himself
No, actually cruel to himself
And everyone besides

The tale of a brotherly bond
Selfish brother
And his brother
Who is unaware

Completely devoid
Of knowledge of the world
Humanity
Women and all that which pertain

The tale of a selfish brother
Who in his selfish way
Protected the brother
Who doesn't know how to be

"The Train"

The train speeds
Like a lightning
Across the vast plain
Along the river
Overflowing
Snow melted
Rain constantly falling
Worried expressions
Those who look outside
Others resigned to quiet
Inside the German train
There sits a girl
In the corner
Munching on her apple
Looking up at the sky
Through the window
Above her head
A blank look
Veiling her thoughts
Desire for less rain
Or more
Who knows
Train speeds faster
And faster
Towards Cologne

"They Danced"

They danced
The man and the blonde
In the stillness of the room
Where all stood by

He was exultant
In her proximity
So delicate
So pure

She danced
The dance
She wanted to dance
Her thoughts adrift

Imagination
Mixed with potential
She wanted to actualize
And realize

In the dance
That revolved in that small space
He hoped
For more of her

She danced
The same dance
But she hoped
For someone else

"Where Are The Flowers?"

Where have all the flowers gone?
Red, white, and blue
Pink and yellow
In this spring day there's none

Rain has fallen
And flowers are downtrodden
Underneath the pressure
And the freaky California weather

There should be sunshine
Pure and radiant
Then California flowers will bloom
And smile in all their glory

But there's only rain
Dreary loss of idealism and virtue
Stripped of hope and possibilities
So flowers hid in their gloom

About the Poet

H. C. Kim is a poet who constantly writes. He has written many books of poetry, including *Transitions: Poems*. He has lived and written poems all over the world – Korea, Israel, England, Germany, and the United States of America. H. C. Kim is the chairperson of Claremont Poetry Club in California, USA.

www.ingramcontent.com/pod-product-compliance
Lightning Source LLC
Chambersburg PA
CBHW031004090426
42737CB00008B/666

* 9 7 8 1 5 9 6 8 9 0 5 7 2 *